the misfits

the magnum photographers

# the misfits

› story of a shoot

arthur miller  serge toubiana

# › CONTENTS

Bruce Davidson photographs John Huston and Arthur Miller deep in discussion. ELLIOTT ERWITT

› SOMETHING BURNING UP

an interview with Arthur Miller *by Serge Toubiana*

Arthur Miller working on his screenplay during filming. Behind the door are Angela Allen, the continuity girl, and John Huston.
BRUCE DAVIDSON

John Huston, Arthur Miller and Clark Gable. HENRI CARTIER-BRESSON

No, I did not know him. Of course, I knew his films ... Marilyn had never played a dramatic part, but John had already directed her in *The Asphalt Jungle*. She felt he was the only director she could work with on a project like this, because it was a much bigger role than anything she had ever done. That's why I called on John. He was interested and, as it turned out, we had wonderful times together. John was a very intelligent man. He had been a writer before he started directing, so he understood the problems of a writer. He knew what the unity of a film, of a play, was. He knew there was more to it than just the unity of images: there had to be a unity of conception. I found I didn't have to teach anything. With many directors, I had to inject a new dimension to the work, which they were not particularly accustomed to. Not all of them, but some. I learnt from John that he would pack the lens with material and let the camera choose. In other words, he'd put a lot of elements in front of the camera and let it find its way. So there's not a lot of cutting from one face to another face in a conversation between two characters. He had them both in the lens. And as a result, I think the film has more inner spirit. When you start chopping up everything, it all becomes physical, and he avoided that. Of course, in those days – the Fifties, that is – there was none of this television-style editing where they seem afraid to keep a shot for more than a split second. That was not done then.

*All in all, you seemed very happy with Huston.*

I loved John. I thought he was terrific. We spent a week or two

in Ireland talking about the movie before we started.

*Was the script complete when the shoot started?*

Yes, it was all written. I made some changes to the last fifteen

minutes of the film, basically to condense some things that had

already been established by then and didn't need to be repeated.

That took a lot of work, and John was a big help there. In the

early parts, we just shot the script.

*About your relationship with Clark Gable: you write in your autobiography that you did not have to speak
to understand each other. Just sitting around with him made for a nice moment.*

Yes, at that point of his life, it was the end of his career.

We did not know ...

*He was still young, barely sixty.*

Yes, but he had been acting for about thirty years, maybe more.

He had seen it all and we were both amused by the same things, so

we did not have to exchange very many words. I know Clark was

very happy with this picture because just before he left the studio

to go hunting – we did not know he was going to die three days

later – he saw the rough cut and he told me, 'This is the best thing

I did in my life.' I don't know if it was true, but he felt it was.

He was pleased with his work and with the making of the film.

*And yet, he had had some doubts before he accepted the part.*

At first, he did not understand the picture, he refused to do it for

months. He would say, 'It's supposed to be a Western, but it's not

a Western!' So I told him, 'It's an Eastern Western ...'

*In a way,* The Misfits *was probably the last Western.*

The last Western! Anyway, his agent, George Chasin – a nice man –

wanted Clark to do the film, and Clark trusted him. That's one

Before a dance scene with Marilyn and Montgomery Clift, Arthur Miller shows her how his father used to dance. EVE ARNOLD
In the middle distance, wearing dark glasses, Paula Strasberg, Marilyn's coach. EVE ARNOLD

reason he finally accepted. Chasin explained to him that while the story was set in the West, it dealt, basically, with a certain philosophical idea that had not occurred to Gable: that of alienation. All these people who literally couldn't subject themselves to a society. And once he had understood that, he agreed to do it, and he loved it, he had a good time doing it.

*In some pictures of the shoot, you look very happy, but not in all of them.*

During most of it, I felt good about it, except that Marilyn was rapidly getting ill. Then it all became difficult because on many days she couldn't work. We had to stop shooting for a week, I think – maybe eight, nine days.

*She left for Los Angeles.*

Before that, it seemed promising. My one disagreement was with the way John was shooting. I might as well tell you, because we discussed it at length. I felt he stayed too close to the actors all the time and we weren't getting that atmosphere of people living on the moon. We were losing their surroundings too often. There should have been more long shots to remind us constantly how isolated these people were, physically and morally. But John did not agree. He claimed we couldn't just film the scenery, while I felt there should have been more long shots of the characters lost in that background. That's the way I saw the film. But I think it probably comes across anyway, that feeling of desolation. Now to answer your question, it's true I look exhausted in some pictures. That's when the trouble began. Of course, my relationship with

13

John Huston, Clark Gable and Montgomery Clift at Harrah's Club, Reno. HENRI CARTIER-BRESSON

Marilyn was deteriorating and I was feeling lonely. Also, I was

simply tired. Some days, we could only shoot an hour or two. So

the frustration was quite severe for everybody. And the heat was

incredible, over 100 degrees Fahrenheit.

*In some photographs, you seem to be a mere spectator …*

By this time, there was not much for me to do. I stayed there in

case John needed some help with Marilyn. I had done everything

I could do, the scriptwriting was finished. Then, as I told you, we

had to stop shooting while she went to her clinic in Los Angeles.

*Did you consider leaving the location at one point?*

John wanted me to stay in case he should want to change

something in the script, and we did make some minor changes

every few days till the end. So, basically, that's why I hung

around, because most of the time there was nothing to do. But

suddenly there would be a crisis of some kind, so I had to be

there. That's the real reason why I stayed on till the end.

*Had you ever spent so much time on a shoot before?*

No.

*And what went through your mind when you saw the movie? What did you think of the adaptation
of your text to the screen?*

I can only compare with the theatre. In the theatre, the word

is everything – to me, anyway. With the cinema, of course, the

image is everything – with a certain amount of indications from

the words, from the dialogue, but they remain secondary. The

primary function of a film is not to deliver speech, so it can't be a

totally satisfactory form for a writer. However, I could see where

I could have gotten hooked by film if I had started younger, perhaps. Because I love the cinema as a form, even though I think it tends to make things a little less profound. I find words more satisfactory. I think they go further, deeper. Although most words aren't very deep. You know, most of the time, the writer's work is rather trivial. We talked about Buñuel before: few books go as deep as his movies. On this particular film, *The Misfits*, I think John finally became exhausted. But he showed remarkable resilience. I could never have kept myself together as he did. The shooting lasted much longer than planned or needed.

*It was scheduled for fifty days and it lasted for ninety.*

Almost twice as much! By that time, we were all wound down. Some of these photographs were taken during that overtime. We no longer passionately believed in the film. But I must say Huston managed to hold the whole thing together. I don't think I could have, I would have given up finally. If I had carried the same responsibility he did, perhaps I would have managed to hang on, but it was a difficult film, and a tragic one, for everybody. You know … soon after, Gable died, and then Monty died. The only one still alive today is Eli Wallach.

*And yet, you had written this story during a happy period of your life.*

Oh, yes! I thought it would be a wonderful adventure. And, in a way, it was; but not as I had expected.

*Could it have been possible for that shoot to go on in happiness and harmony?*

No, it couldn't have been. Because after all, even though it ends on a note of hopefulness, the story is basically tragic in its attitude

15

toward the country and toward itself. *The Misfits'* characters are

disconnected, and they represent a lot of people who have

superficial connections but profoundly feel they are not connected.

So this atmosphere was bound to spread beyond the film itself,

I think.

*Do you think Huston felt that while he was making the picture?*

John himself was like that, he had no real connections with

anybody.

*The legend says he was a player.*

Yes, he was. A good one too, but he was a player.

*These pictures have been taken at the studio. Does that mean it was the end of the shoot?*

It must have been in Hollywood, possibly the last day. We had

only two days' work in the studio. By then, I was completely

distant from the whole thing. They all seem very distant from me.

*Do you remember discussing Marilyn's character with her? Was it possible?*

No, we wouldn't talk. Her 'coach', Paula Strasberg, she was there

constantly, so that John got really mad at one point and insisted

that she didn't speak to him or to Marilyn anymore. Because by

this time, he had to talk to the coach to communicate with

Marilyn. She was completely distressed, so the coach was the

interpreter. It was as if they spoke two different languages, and

I always blamed the coach for that.

*Why?*

Marilyn was in such need of security ... And there are deeper

reasons. That coach was a little crazy, she was an opportunist,

I thought, and not competent to help.

*A sort of guru?*

Yes, a guru. And people like that were very attracted to Marilyn,

Marilyn Monroe with her coach, Paula Strasberg. INGE MORATH

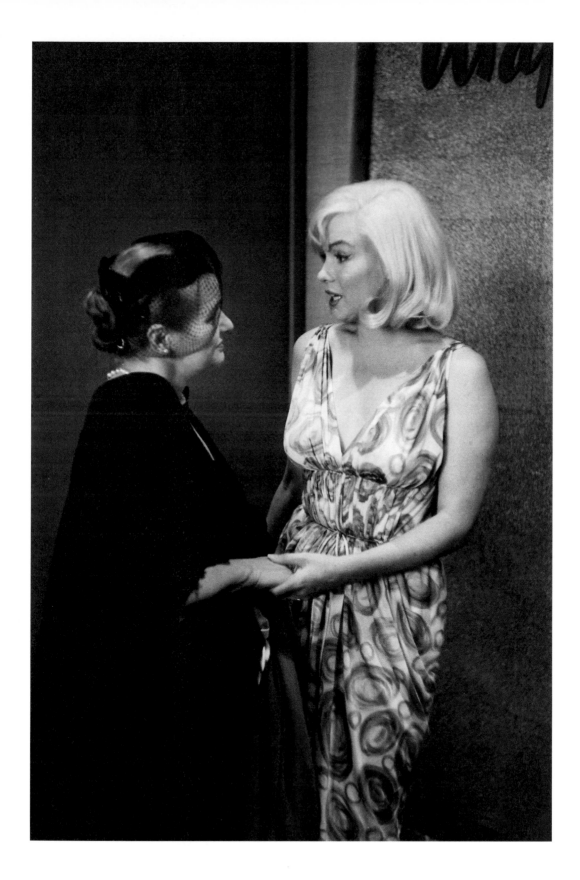

Marilyn Monroe and Arthur Miller in their hotel room. INGE MORATH

and she to them, very often. In fact, I think Marilyn believed in

Lee Strasberg, and that woman was a kind of deputy conveying

his great wisdom. Everybody else was locked out of their

arrangement. Huston himself could not get through to Marilyn.

And I was simply out of it toward that part of the shooting.

*Was Paula Strasberg imposed on the shoot by contract?*

Sure, she had to be there on Marilyn's insistence. On a Fox film,

she even made more money than Marilyn.

*How do you analyze that? Do you think Marilyn was so insecure she needed a strong woman by her side?*

Yes, she had a need for an older woman who could weave

fantasies around her. But Paula was not helpful: she played the

part of a guru, a power Marilyn had given to her, of course,

because she was the wife and deputy of the great Lee Strasberg.

Occasionally, they spoke with him on the phone, which increased

her isolation from John and all the others – except Paula. But

Paula had nothing to give Marilyn that could help her, except to

reaffirm her suspicions about others. That was her function, to

confirm Marilyn's anxieties. I remember this picture. Inge took it.

[Arthur Miller looks at a photograph taken in Marilyn's bedroom: she and Miller are

several metres apart] We were apart by then.

*There was no more intimacy between you?*

No.

*You had written that part for Marilyn as a sort of gift. Then it went all wrong. But the movie still exists.*

Ironically, yes. But there it is, it still exists. That's the great thing

about the films. It's different with the theatre.

*In the memories ...*

Yes, but most people don't remember. No, that's the wonderful

part of it, she goes on and on playing that part ...

20

John Huston directing Marilyn on location at Pyramid Lake, Nevada. ERNST HAAS

Montgomery Clift, Marilyn Monroe and Clark Gable. ERICH HARTMANN

*Do you think all that had to happen for the film to exist? That something had to be lost?*

Yes, maybe that's necessary. I don't think so, but apparently it is.

*Inge, do you remember these photographs precisely?*

INGE MORATH: I remember very well. I was so naive, I tried to make them pose together, but it was impossible. I was working at the same time as Henri Cartier-Bresson, remember? He had finally managed to get a rendezvous with both of you, but Marilyn did not want to ...

ARTHUR MILLER: Marilyn liked Inge very, very much.

MORATH: Yes, she did. I liked her too. I didn't want anything from her. I had already photographed many stars, but she was always so sweet ...

I saw what happened on the set, but I don't think about that.

*Looking at all those pictures of Marilyn, I get the feeling she could change within a second, be a child, an adult, funny or profound.*

MORATH: It's true.

[Speaking to Arthur Miller] She really knew you didn't like Paula.

MILLER: Oh, I couldn't stand that woman! Nobody could! The crew nicknamed her 'Black Bart' because she always wore black. You see, Strasberg pretended to have some secret key to heaven, and that's how he manipulated actors. In fact, you can do that with lots of people. Somebody assumes authority and nobody knows why. My reaction is just the opposite: I can't give authority that way to someone else, so I couldn't have peaceful relations with that person. Anyway, I thought Strasberg was a very destructive force. He tried to make himself indispensable to the actors, whereas a real coach should try to make them independent. Strasberg worked the opposite way.

23

While on location in Nevada, John Huston spent long hours, sometimes whole nights, at the gaming tables in Reno. Marilyn went with him once, toward the end of filming. EVE ARNOLD

When Marilyn asked Huston how to throw the dice, he replied: 'Don't think about it, honey, just throw. That's the story of your life. Don't think, do it.' EVE ARNOLD

Yes, but not as many as he liked to make you think. He always claimed credit for Marlon Brando's success. But Brando was probably three times in his life in the Actors' Studio! The legend also has it that he created the Actors' Studio, but in fact it's Elia Kazan who founded that acting school. Anyway, it's all history now ...

*Did Huston direct the actors much?*

From my point of view, not enough, very often. I would have interfered more. I think John was more interested in the image, in the pictorial aspect. He expected the actors to be themselves, he didn't interfere very much with their interpretation. But I never heard him say anything about that. He was a gentleman, never losing his temper, even in the most difficult situations, where he would just get a little tougher, but not personal. I have been told he was different when he worked with Montgomery Clift.

He hated him, for reasons I never knew. But I did not see that on *The Misfits*. Huston was kind and considerate. But perhaps he was different on different films.

*In several photographs Huston is gambling in a casino.*

He loved to gamble. One night, he lost twenty-five thousand dollars, which he didn't have, of course. John used to spend his money as soon as he got it. The gangsters who ran the place told him politely he was never going to leave town unless he paid that bill. So, one evening, I left him around nine o'clock after dinner at this table. [Miller points to one photo] I believe it was this table ...

I came down the next morning around six, and there he was. He had made his money back! Plus about five hundred or a thousand dollars! He stayed up at it the whole night. Then he goes on location and falls asleep. When he woke up, he said, 'Okay! We deal with scene number nine' or whatever. And the script girl answered, 'But we did that one yesterday!' It was totally crazy. I'll never forget that one.

*You talked about the sensation of being on the moon.*
Yes, I don't know, it must be different today. But at the time, some people went there who were divorced or felt alienated from the big city. They were looking for something, they didn't know what. The whole state was full of misfits, people who did not fit anywhere. They knew it, they made fun of it, of their inability to function in the United States. For example, there was a woman who had divorced ten years before. She had come from New York for that purpose and she stayed on … Every year, her former husband would send her a rose for her birthday, and that one flower made her so happy. She had nothing else in life, but she thought that was okay.

*Tell me about Frank Taylor, the producer. Was* The Misfits *his first production?*
Frank had been my publisher in the past. Marilyn needed somebody who would simply be friendly with her. Frank had worked at the Fox studios, but through no fault of his own he had never produced anything there. None of his projects ever came off. He wanted to adapt Faulkner, Fitzgerald, great writers, and at the

time, of course, nobody was interested. But he worked there for

some years before going back to publishing. Once the script of

*The Misfits* was finished, I called and asked him to be the producer

and, of course, he jumped at that. He loved the idea, he was a

sweet man, a very nice man.

*Did he produce other movies after* The Misfits?

I think he stopped, as far as I know. He went back to the

publishing business.

*There's a story connected with this photo, taken by Elliott Erwitt. All the Magnum photographers present during the shoot tried to get a picture of the whole crew. He's the only one who managed to do it. It looks like a family picture, but the family was already destroyed, right?*

Right. It's sad. They were all misfits! It's a good title.

*What was the relationship between Marilyn and Montgomery Clift during the shoot?*

As far as I could tell, Marilyn and Monty were friends, with great

respect for one another.

*Huston didn't trust him?*

The insurance company had refused to insure Monty. His

drinking, I suppose. But John got him insured because he felt he

was perfect for the part ... But he was worried, because by then

Monty was drinking on his film. But on *Misfits*, Monty turned out

to be the most reliable person of the whole lot! [Laughs]

Well, you never know.

*I like that picture of Clark Gable: it's the image of a star, but he seems exhausted.*

He was exhausted. The heat was so unbearable, and Clark had to

wear heavy clothes to protect his skin when he was being dragged

by the horses.

*Why do you think Marilyn loved being photographed so much?*

It depended very much on how she felt about herself. She liked

Inge because she thought Inge was kind. But she was very unhappy

when people were aggressive with her.

Clark Gable. EVE ARNOLD

[Miller looks at a picture]

She has a wonderful expression there. Do you know the story behind this picture?

[Miller shows a photo of Marilyn dancing around a tree, a scene in *The Misfits*]

Well, in those days, the Catholic Church in New York had to preview the films, otherwise they could condemn them. So the priests saw the movie, and they did not like it. So we had a meeting. What was the problem? It was one of the worst they ever had faced, they said: for them, in the scene where Marilyn dances around a tree, she was masturbating. Can you believe it? They wanted it to be cut. I told them not only we would not cut it, but if you persist, I'll report our whole conversation to *The New York Times*. That was the end of it. [Laughter]

*Does the movie resemble what you imagined when you were writing it?*

Yes and no. As I said, I had thought the film would give a feeling of more isolation. Of course, I understand the camera has to come closer to the actors to film the dialogues. I had never thought of that when I was writing. So I didn't expect so many close-ups. I had visualized the whole thing as though from a distance. I had spent time out there, I lived there for a couple months. The space is so vast, oppressive, you're lost in it, you can spend a whole day without seeing anybody, not a car, nothing. I wanted to get that feeling from the film. Apart from that, I think it did appear like what I expected. The big question in my mind was whether we

The scene where Marilyn dances around a tree. INGE MORATH

were taking advantage of that desolation or not, and I still don't
know if the movie could have been different shot another way, if
John had directed it differently. I think there are only two or three
shots from a distance – of the wild horses filmed from the plane –
but that's about it. For instance, today it's honky-tonks, hotels and
God knows what, but in those days, there was not a soul around
Pyramid Lake. It was still an Indian reservation, exactly the way
it was when God made the world. Well, there are no wide shots of
it in the film, except a medium one where Marilyn steps out of the
water. There's a moonlike quality to that lake, its water is salty
and it holds fish nowhere else to be found, except for one other
lake in India, and nobody knows why they occur only in those two
lakes. They're ancient fossil species, terribly ugly, hundreds of
thousands of years old. That feeling should have gotten into the
film. There's an irony between these people loving each other
against that death, but we did not get that presence of death.
I didn't feel it. To me, it does not come across; you get it from
the dialogues, and in some situations, but I'm not sure. What do
you think?

*No, that's not the way I felt when I saw the film.*

Maybe I'm wrong. I wish we had gone more that way. But,
altogether, I always felt it's a fascinating movie. And, under the
circumstances, I don't know another director who would have
done it as beautifully.

*In the Hollywood system an author rarely originates a project. Yet not only did you write the story, you followed through the making of the film from beginning to end. That's unusual.*

Normally it's impossible. In that case, of course, there was the fact Marilyn wanted to do the film and she was a big star. Otherwise, it probably would have been different. But at the same time, I had already published *The Misfits* as a short story, so I was the only one who knew anything about this. It was not an easy subject that the studios could give for adaptation to some writers. And, by the way, whatever is good or bad in the film, I think it has a certain underlying unity coming from the fact it's one man's work, one man's idea, rather than the product of a committee of a dozen different producers or screenwriters.

*It was a kind of an independent film within the system, don't you think?*

Even then, it was a very unusual situation. Huston was a big-name director, yet there was always some producer watching over him to keep a measure of control. I am not even sure he got the final cut on all his movies. There was no interference whatsoever with that one. But then, we were working for United Artists. That was already Greenwich Village. These people had genuine aesthetic interest. They were not only businessmen.

*Did filming in black and white raise a problem?*

I'm sure the studios didn't want black and white, because colour was already used for most films. As far as I remember, it was not my idea, but I liked it. Filming that area in colour would have made the scenery look too soft on screen, too pretty. It wouldn't have looked like drying bones, which is what it actually looks like. In colour, they would be a little pink, a little green, a little yellow.

Montgomery Clift. ERNST HAAS

Marilyn Monroe. BRUCE DAVIDSON

35

That's not bones anymore. John wanted black and white. He was

a painter by instinct. I think his sensibility told him black and

white belonged with this story. He was right about that, and I was

very happy with it.

*Is it true that, at first, Marilyn refused the part?*

I think she wouldn't have made the film if John had not directed it.

Mainly because it was a tremendous challenge for her. She felt she

would need help, and Huston would control and help her. He was

the only director who had previously been respectful and treated

her like an actress. She dreaded winding up in the hands of one of

these others. It had to be a Hollywood director who did not expect

some kitsch from her, who would confront the tragedy of the story

without twisting it around to make it more pleasant for the public.

She knew that John would carry it through, and so did I. If he had

not done the movie, she would probably have accepted two, three

other directors, but she was scared to play in such a film. She was

not sure at all she could handle it even under John's direction.

*But you knew she could.*

Yes. Marilyn was far more intelligent than they all gave her credit

for, because she gave the impression of a light-headed comedian.

And she was a marvellous comic actress. But she wanted to play

some serious roles, without being confident she could do it. She

was afraid not to be taken seriously. Of course, John believed she

could be because he had taken her seriously from the start, in *The*

*Asphalt Jungle*. That was the reassurance she desperately needed.

*Do you remember how the film was received by the critics?*
They did not know what to make of it. Why? First, here was a comedy actress in a tragic part. Second, here was a movie with Western people and it was not a Western. So what could it be? They didn't know what to expect. The story took place in Reno, so they counted on gambling, prostitutes, horse races and all the usual stuff in that kind of movie. Then, they heard conversations such as they never heard from such characters before. A few critics were positive about the picture, but most of them were simply baffled. And I am sure they thought it was going to disappear within a week and be a failure. Financially, it probably was at the beginning. Later on, I'm sure they made money on it. I understand it's often shown on TV. I don't get anything from it, but maybe some people do.

*Was Marilyn pleased with the film?*
[Pause]

I really don't know. I couldn't tell you. By then, we were hardly able to speak to each other, and I was not with her at the screening. I don't know what she made of it. I never found out.

*Can this film be seen, in some way, as a documentary on Marilyn Monroe?*
Actually, the character was based on a different woman, but that does not matter. I agree with you she was so much like Roslyn; but for that kind of person, who cannot get connected, Nevada was the perfect place, because people like that are all over the place.

*That's why the scene where Roslyn communicates with the trees, with nature, is so moving.*
Exactly, with the earth, with nature ...

*What human beings don't understand is that it's communication on a totally different level.*
They all want to communicate, but they don't dare because it would limit their freedom.

37

The desert at Pyramid Lake, Nevada. Arthur Miller was very taken with its lunar landscape: 'I felt there should have been more long shots of the characters lost in that background.' ERNST HAAS

'In those days, there was not a soul around Pyramid Lake. It was still an Indian reservation, exactly the way it was when God made the world.' ERNST HAAS

*There's a modern ecological dimension to the film, with Roslyn begging the men to spare the horses*
*and protect nature. She is on the side of life, which she sees in everything, while the men are on the side of death.*

I had written another story before I wrote *The Misfits*. It had

nothing to do with this one. It was about a woman walking with

her husband on a beach where fishermen are pulling in their nets

and throwing the fish they don't want on the sand to die. So that

woman runs around to throw them back in the sea and it amuses

the fishermen. The story is called 'Please Don't Kill Anything'.

*You started writing* The Misfits *in 1956, and the film was finished in 1960. That's about four years.*

Yes, something like that. I had started writing it on Long Island.

*But you spent six weeks in Nevada, you saw the country, you met people there.*

Yes. In fact, one day, we were shooting a scene with Gable saying

his lines to the camera, I turned around and suddenly here was one

of the cowboys who had told me the same things two years before,

and, of course, he made no connection whatsoever between himself

and Gable's character. I knew several men like him while I was in

Reno. They just ran after horses, caught them and sold them. The

whole thing was so ridiculous. But man is a hunter. Nevada is a

very dry territory. The grass is so sparse they need a hundred acres

to feed one cow. When the horses come in, the ranchers aren't very

happy because they eat the cows' grass. So they shoot the horses.

I don't know if they still do and get away with it today, because

of public consciousness, but they certainly did that before.

Actually, the film was really about the total alienation of people

from contemporary technology. They tried to escape technology,

to stay away from that and still have relationships with their fellow

humans. Very difficult. I worship people who know how to deal with horses, with the land, but they're not all alike: some worship people who make a lot of money. Once, I was in the desert with some cowboys. We came upon a little shack, hardly bigger than this room, that cowboys used to rest. Absolutely nothing within fifty miles, just that one little building, and on the floor there were girlie magazines and some about guitar-playing cowboys too.

I discovered they believed those cowboys were the real ones, and not them. They were not something called 'cowboys', they were just working men. Reality was in the movies. It was terrible.

I remember feeling it was the end of human consciousness that they should devalue themselves and value this nonsense. Because the world didn't respect them, the realities, but respected the facsimiles, they were nothing.

*Having seen* The Misfits *many times, I can feel it's a Huston film, but yours as well. Each brought his own contribution.*

Yes, but it's something unpredictable and out of one's control. I can understand it, but I didn't engineer the picture for that. It's like several planets revolving around one another. I never know what will result from a script or a stage play. A lot also depends on the actors. I didn't know who they would be when I wrote *The Misfits.* It so happened they were all wonderful.

*Did Huston choose them?*

Yes, but not only Huston. There was also sheer luck, there were the agents. For instance, Clark's agent was with MCA, the agency that represented me. Of course, I thought Gable would be

wonderful in the film, but in fact he probably got the part because we were with the same agency. They were the first ones to get the script, so they knew immediately who they wanted for the roles. Getting Monty was also their idea, but it was John's too. A lot of luck was involved, just as it happens in life. You meet the right person, or the wrong one, and there's no way to explain it.

*After this film, did you feel like writing for the cinema again?*

No, because writing for the cinema, as I would do it, takes at least a year. More likely, to get everything settled, it's over a year. Furthermore, it's an industry. Whoever decides to put in the money, you're never going to meet that guy. You see, when I write a play, I know it will go on stage. So devoting so much time without even knowing if the film will be done ... is too depressing. Moreover, I originate everything I write. I never wrote anything somebody else said was a good idea. I belong to the old generation of writers who did everything themselves from beginning to end, before the invention of those committees who avail themselves of other people's projects. When we did *Death of a Salesman* on Broadway with Dustin Hoffman, CBS organized a big dinner for us and asked me to make a speech. They were very happy because they had gotten a TV film from the stage production. I asked them, 'What can I tell you? This whole thing was cooked up by one man. No committees.' Silence. 'All the decisions were made by that man. Then he brought in another man, the director. The two made more

Marilyn Monroe and Arthur Miller. BRUCE DAVIDSON

decisions, then they brought in the actors, and they made some

additional decisions, and that's how this thing got made.' Then

I sat down. They were not happy with my speech because they all

depend upon interfering with the creative process they think they

have originated. That's why I don't like the movies as an artist.

However, if I were a director, which I could have been – whether

you are Buñuel or any ordinary fellow, you must be very

diplomatic and very clever and deal with these authorities because

they have the money to make the film.

*The shooting of* The Misfits *must be a strange memory for you.*

It's both sad and happy. What's very sad, as you found out, is that

I had written it to make Marilyn feel good. And for her, it resulted

in complete collapse. But at the same time, I am glad it was done,

because her dream was to be a serious actress.

*Today, everybody agrees she was.*

True. And everybody considers this role as a big leap in her career.

Frankly, if I had not written it and if she had not played that part,

I question whether she would ever have done anything

comparable, anything that serious. Of course, she was marvellous

simply as a comedian. In *Some Like It Hot*, for instance, she was

fantastic. And, to me, it's work just as serious and calling for as

much intelligence and talent as a dramatic part. But I think even

though she had such difficulty making *The Misfits*, it had nothing

to do with John or with me. She was scared, she was frightened.

She barely could get herself to face the camera.

*Do you think this movie is more cruel than many others?*

Yes, I think so. I can't recall witnessing such cruelty in the theatre,

where the tradition is more to a certain 'gentillesse'.

*There is something burning up, something that consumes the actors in that film.*

Maybe that's what makes us go so much higher, the reward is so

much greater in the movies. You become famous throughout the

world, you become rich, and so on. That does not happen in the

theatre. Certainly not in our time, not anymore. If you do a good

job in the theatre, people appreciate ... and goodbye. You're

certainly not going to get rich in the theatre. An actor can do a

fantastic job, but compared to the film salaries!

*A certain cruelty is inherent in the star system, don't you think?*

Oh, yes! They all paid for it, every one on this picture.

[Showing a photograph] This guy paid, too – Gable was a chain

smoker, one cigarette after the other. There was high nervousness

in all the scenes. Maybe it's like that on all shoots ...

*Men or women, stars spend their time waiting between takes. It's a bizarre, very passive situation, isn't it?*

It's an infant's position. That's why many male stars or actors

resent it. They want to be producers or directors, because it is in

the nature of the actor's work to be deprived of any control.

This interview took place 3 XII 1998 at the home of Inge Morath and Arthur Miller in Roxbury, Connecticut.

A 'sad and happy' memory. Arthur Miller during the shoot. BRUCE DAVIDSON

The mustangs, the 'misfit' horses, were equally the heroes of the film. Once a symbol of the Wild West, now they were destined to end up as dog food. ERNST HAAS

› BLACK DESERT, WHITE DESERT

essay *by Serge Toubiana*

In his autobiography, *Timebends: A Life*, Arthur Miller describes the origins
of *The Misfits* at some length. The theme first appeared as a short story
published in the American magazine *Esquire* in October 1957. It was written
after Miller had had to spend some time in Nevada in the spring of 1956
while waiting for a divorce from his first wife. Nevada law is notoriously lax,
and the state will grant a divorce to anyone who has lived there for six weeks
or more. Miller had rented a cabin at Pyramid Lake, tucked away about a
hundred miles from Reno, the nearest city, where he would go once a week
or so to do his shopping and get his laundry done. One of his neighbours
was Saul Bellow, who was there for similar reasons. The Nevada desert
provided Miller with the figures who were to be the heroes of his story:
cowboys rather adrift in the modern world, free-spirited men who lived an
outdoor life, making a living by catching wild horses they would then sell
to be made into dog food. He was interested in the way they lived on the
margins of society, outside the community. One day, two of the cowboys
invited him to join their hunt for wild horses. With them was a younger man,
who remained completely silent. Miller studied these men closely as they used
lassos to catch the mustangs, then tethered them to large tyres to prevent
them escaping. He later described Pyramid Lake as 'a gray salty lake miles
long, surrounded by a Paiute Indian reservation, a forbidding but beautiful
place occasionally favored by movie companies shooting scenes of weird
monsters in outer space'.[1]

While Miller was living in Nevada waiting to obtain his divorce and marry Marilyn Monroe, she was in Hollywood, making *Bus Stop* with director Joshua Logan. She was experiencing great difficulty in advancing her Hollywood career; to her despair, producers would only cast her as a sexy ingénue in lightweight comedies, denying her parts worthy of her talent. She was under contract to Twentieth Century Fox and had to fulfil her commitments before setting up her own production company, Marilyn Monroe Productions, with her associate, photographer Milton Greene. This move was intended to free her from the studios, as Norman Rosten, Miller's friend, confirms when he describes how, after the success of *The Seven Year Itch*, she tried to renegotiate the terms of her contract with Fox to give herself higher fees and, above all, a say on scripts and choice of directors: 'She had sensed her power; she was determined to test it. She was ready to enter the fray, to deal with the lawyers, press agents, promotion people: in short to deal.'[2] Marilyn cherished hopes of finding more dignified parts, despite the frequent jibes aimed at her in the American popular press. In his autobiography, Miller describes 'the then powerful movie columnists ... taking shots at Marilyn, the non-actor floozy, for the proposterous chutzpah of making demands on so great and noble a corporation as Twentieth Century Fox'. At this point, Marilyn was trying to change her way of life and be a good wife while she waited to be offered a 'wonderful film'. Her marriage to Miller in Connecticut on 1 July 1956 was expected to help her distance herself from the studios. After the wedding, the couple moved to

New York, and Marilyn again took courses at the Actors' Studio, where Lee Strasberg was teaching his 'Method', based on Stanislavsky's theory of acting. There she made friends with Eli Wallach, with whom she would later appear in *The Misfits*.

One of the first projects of Marilyn Monroe Productions was *The Prince and the Showgirl*, an adaptation of Terence Rattigan's comedy, directed by and starring Laurence Olivier. Marilyn was thrilled to be playing opposite a great actor like Olivier, but their relationship on the set at Shepperton studios was strained, and the film was a disappointment. Miller, however, took advantage of this interlude to write his short story, *The Misfits*.

## AN OFFERING FOR MARILYN

After making *The Prince and the Showgirl*, Marilyn Monroe and Arthur Miller returned to set up home in New York, spending weekends at a rented house by the sea on Long Island. In the summer of 1957, Marilyn, who wanted a child, found she was pregnant. But the pregnancy was ectopic, and she was rushed to hospital in New York. Her friend Sam Shaw, who had started taking photographs of her at the beginning of the 1950s when she was relatively unknown, came to visit her. At the hospital, he met Miller, whose *Esquire* story he had read. While they were taking a walk together, he suggested that Miller turn it into a screenplay: 'It would make a great movie and that's a woman's part she could kick into the stands.' Miller, who had previously seemed reluctant to work in the cinema, liked the idea and immediately got down to work. He wanted Marilyn to have a part written

Marilyn learning her lines with Paula Strasberg. DENNIS STOCK

especially for her that would show the studio bosses she had the makings of an intelligent and sensitive actress with a gift for serious drama. *The Misfits* was his offering to her at a time when she had just suffered a terrible ordeal – she now knew she would never be able to have children – and was in open conflict with Fox over the direction her career should take. Her contract required that she complete two other films: *Some Like It Hot*, the second film in which she was to be directed by Billy Wilder (and a runaway success); and immediately afterwards, *Let's Make Love*, directed by George Cukor, in which she would play opposite Yves Montand.

In its first version, as a short story, three male characters of different ages dominate *The Misfits*: Guido, the pilot; Gay Langland, the hunter of wild horses; and Perce Howland, a young rodeo rider and a bit of a daredevil. Roslyn, the female character, hardly appears; she is Gay's wife, but they are separated. Miller summarizes it as follows: 'a story of three men who cannot locate a home on the earth for themselves and who, for something to do, catch wild horses to go to be butchered for dog food, and a woman, as homeless as they, but whose intact sense of life's sacredness suggests a meaning for existence. It was a story about the indifference I had been feeling not only in Nevada, but in the world now. We were being stunned at our powerlessness to control our lives, and Nevada was simply the perfection of our common loss.'

The character of Roslyn in *The Misfits* could be Marilyn's double. DENNIS STOCK

One of the paradoxes of *The Misfits* is that Marilyn Monroe hesitated for a long time before agreeing to play the part of Roslyn. 'She read parts of the screenplay and laughed delightedly at some of the cowboys' lines,' says Miller, 'but seemed to withhold full commitment to playing Roslyn.' She probably thought Roslyn was too similar to herself, almost her double, with the same problems, the same worries, the same difficulty in coping with life. Indeed, as Miller wrote the screenplay he was observing the woman who was now living with him, and who, although she had a new life and felt more protected, was as vulnerable as ever, ceaselessly struggling with the dark forces that prevented her personality blossoming. 'Her very pain bespoke life and the wrestling with the angel of death. She was a living rebuke to anyone who didn't care,' wrote Miller. Like Marilyn, Roslyn had a difficult childhood and a troubled relationship with her mother, compounded of intimacy and rejection, and they share the same anxieties and loneliness, the same feeling of abandonment and a childlike wonder where children or animals are concerned. But their ingenuous admiration turns into mistrust as soon as a man gets too close and falls in love in them. After her divorce, which comes right at the beginning of the film, Roslyn looks for a place in the world where she can be happy, while knowing in her heart of hearts that happiness is impossible. She meets the three cowboys and has a love affair with Gay Langland (played by Clark Gable), who is both lover and father-figure. After many ordeals, most notably the climactic scene in the middle of the desert when Roslyn begs the cowboys to release the wild horses, *The Misfits* ends on a note of hope as Roslyn responds to a question ('Would you ever want a kid with me?') that Gay asked her in an earlier scene: 'If there could be one person in the world, a child who could be brave from the beginning … I was scared to when you asked me, but I'm not so much now.'

It was not long before the idea of submitting the script to John Huston emerged. Miller realized that this was a clinching argument in persuading Marilyn to agree to appear in the film; he was convinced that Marilyn would feel at ease with Huston. He had already told the story of *The Misfits* to an old friend, Frank Taylor, playing all the roles and even imitating the language of the Nevada cowboys. Taylor insisted on reading the script, and loved it. The two had known each other for years; Taylor (and Miller's first wife) had worked for a company called Reynal and Hitchcock, who had published Miller's early books, *Situation Normal* and the novel *Focus*. In the late 1940s, Taylor joined Twentieth Century Fox, hoping to develop film projects for them, including an adaptation of F. Scott Fitzgerald's *Tender is the Night*. Taylor, whom Miller describes as 'a gaunt, sophisticated man of great height … an imaginative mix of aggressive entrepreneur and aficionado of literature', eagerly agreed to produce the film for Seven Arts Productions, a subsidiary of United Artists. The idea of approaching Huston to direct the film probably came out of discussions between Miller and Taylor; Taylor was fortunate enough to know him personally.

The lovers in *The Misfits*. Clark Gable as Gay to Marilyn Monroe as Roslyn: 'Honey, we've all got to go sometime, reason or no reason. Dying's as natural as living. A man who's too afraid to die is too afraid to live.' CORNELL CAPA

On 14 July 1958, before the screenplay was actually completed, Miller wrote
to Huston, who was staying at his Irish country home, St Clerans, in Galway,
offering to send him the script. He summed up his project briefly: 'The setting
is the Nevada back country, concerns two cowboys, a pilot, a girl, and the
last of the mustangs up in the mountains ... The script is an early draft.
If you are interested I'd want to sit and talk over my notions of further
developments and of course would like to hear yours.'3 Knowing that
Huston had decided for the time being not to work in the United States –
probably for tax reasons – Miller was careful to reassure him: 'Having seen
so much of the earth, perhaps you'll know of a foreign locale equivalent if,
in fact, it's impossible to work here.' Nine days later, on 23 July, Huston
replied: 'I was delighted to get your letter and flattered that you should have
thought to write to me about your script. Do send it on to me right and you
shall hear from me about it immediately. It's true that for various reasons
I prefer to do pictures outside of the United States for the present time, but
making a good picture is much more important. There are, however, parts
of Mexico that are identical to northern Nevada – even in wintertime.'

While Marilyn was filming *Some Like It Hot* with Billy Wilder, Miller
worked on his script. On 16 June 1959, he sent a new draft to Huston, who
was in London. 'Dear John, here is the beginning of the screenplay. I ought
to say nothing about it until you had read it. One or two purely mechanical
exchanges of dialogue are merely summarized, but the rest is fully written

out. I hope to hear from you soon, and was sorry to learn that you were not coming to New York this week. I have become newly enamored with the whole story... but this time not so exclusively from a telescopic distance. I think they are people now and that this tale can break an audience's heart. I am going on with the revision because I have a great lust for it now.' Miller spent the whole summer polishing the screenplay, and sent Huston an almost final version in late September. Finally, on 29 September, Huston was able to send him an enthusiastic telegram in New York: 'Dear Arthur, script magnificent. Regards, John.'

At this time, Huston was working on an ambitious project to make a film on the life of Freud, based on a screenplay by Jean-Paul Sartre. But he found Sartre's first draft too 'literary', especially as it ran to several hundred pages. Miller's proposal came just at the right time – it would be several months before shooting could start on the *Freud* project, and Huston was far from sorry at the prospect of working with Marilyn Monroe again. Ten years previously, in 1949, he had put her through screen tests when he was preparing to make *We Were Strangers* for Columbia. 'She used to come to the set and watch the shooting ... There was some talk of Columbia giving her a screen test. She was a very pretty girl, young and appealing, but so are thousands of girls in Hollywood. Such talk often leads to the casting couch rather than to the studio floor, and I suspected someone was setting her up. Something about Marilyn elicited my protectiveness, so, to forestall any hanky-panky, I expressed my readiness to do a test, in color, with John

Garfield playing opposite her.'4 The following year, when he was about to make *The Asphalt Jungle* and was looking for an actress to play Angela, the pretty mistress of the shady lawyer played by Louis Calhern, he remembered her. This screen test was a success. 'The scene she was to read called for Angela to be stretched out on a divan; there was no divan in my office, so Marilyn said, "I'd like to do the scene on the floor"… And that's the way she did it. She kicked off her shoes, lay down on the floor and read for us. When she finished, Arthur [Hornblow, the producer of the film] and I looked at each other and nodded. She was Angela to a "T".' Meanwhile, between her debut in *The Asphalt Jungle* and the shooting of *The Misfits*, Marilyn had become one of Hollywood's biggest stars. Huston, also under contract to Fox, had the reputation of being a maverick and an adventurer, a great gambler who alternated between commercial successes and disasters, a good director of actors with the useful attribute of being able to adapt to any situation.

A STAR-STUDDED FILM ON THE MARGINS OF THE HOLLYWOOD SYSTEM

Lew Wasserman, the powerful head of the MCA agency to which Marilyn Monroe and Arthur Miller were both under contract, put his whole weight behind the project. Thanks to him, Miller and Taylor were able to assemble a dream cast that fitted perfectly the choices they had originally made. At one time, they had considered Robert Mitchum for the part of Gay Langland. Elliott Hyman, head of Seven Arts, contacted him, and he seemed interested in reading the screenplay, but did not get in touch again. On 13 November 1959, Clark Gable met Miller, who talked to him about the project, and

'I tell an actor as little as I possibly can. When I have to step in, I feel defeated', John Huston. EVE ARNOLD

especially about the character of Langland. Gable was very puzzled at first and wondered just what kind of a script it was: a Western, or something else? Miller found a definition that settled the question: 'It's a sort of Eastern Western.' After that, Gable felt ready to take the plunge.

With Montgomery Clift, on the other hand, whom they had in mind for the part of Perce, the problem was that no insurance company would cover him after the terrible car accident that had disfigured his face and intensified his self-destructive impulses. But Miller and Huston insisted on having him, and they eventually won the insurers over. Both of them were very happy with the way Clift behaved throughout the shoot, as well as with his moving portrayal of Perce. He is extraordinarily powerful in two of the film's most affecting scenes: in the first, a monologue, he calls his mother from a phone box at the side of the road just before arriving in Dayton to ride in a rodeo; in the second, lying stretched out on the floor in the back room of a saloon, he confides in Roslyn, his head resting on her knees. When these scenes were shot, Clift was word-perfect; his fellow-actors and the whole crew were amazed. The parts of Isabelle, Roslyn's landlady in Reno, and the pilot were played by Thelma Ritter and Eli Wallach, two good film actors who had also acted on the New York stage.

From its origins to its production, *The Misfits* seems like an independent film, conceived in a completely different way from the traditional studio system. The impulse behind it belonged entirely to Miller, the screenwriter, an unusual state of affairs in American cinema, where the initiative always came

*Above:* Arthur Miller with John Huston. ELLIOTT ERWITT
*Below:* With Frank Taylor, the producer. EVE ARNOLD

exclusively from the producers. But the presence of Marilyn Monroe and Clark Gable was enough to guarantee finance for the film, whose initial budget was three and a half million dollars, a reasonable sum for Hollywood at that time, given also that Monroe's and Gable's fees accounted for a significant part of it.

An atypical production like *The Misfits* was possible at the beginning of the 1960s because the industry was going through a serious crisis caused by the first effects of competition from television. The studios started investing heavily in producing TV series, and many film sets were requisitioned or adapted to the needs of the new medium. It was, therefore, a good moment for experimentation on the fringes of the big studio economy. The same year, Hitchcock made *Psycho*, an experiment carried out 'under the same conditions as a television show',5 with a budget of only 800,000 dollars.

The plan was that *The Misfits* would be shot almost entirely out of doors, in the places in Reno and the Nevada desert where Miller had had the idea for the story and had come across his characters. Russell Metty, one of Hollywood's most respected cameramen, was responsible for lighting it in black and white, at a time when most studio productions, specifically to counteract the growing influence of television, were shot in colour and in CinemaScope. From that point of view also, the aesthetic assumptions behind *The Misfits*, close to those of documentary, went against the grain of the traditional star vehicle. Other members of the crew were chosen from among the best technical people. They included George Tomasini, Hitchcock's regular editor; 'Doc' Erickson, the production manager, who had also worked with Hitchcock; and Steve Grimes, the art director. And when big stars are involved, it always entails additional personnel. Marilyn, for example, had her coach, Paula Strasberg (the wife of Lee Strasberg), with her throughout the shoot, as well as her personal secretary, May Reis; her masseur; her regular make-up artist; her hairdresser; her lighting stand-in; a dresser and a chauffeur. In that respect, *The Misfits* was a film like any other, except for the fact that it was to be made in high summer in the desert, far away from Hollywood and in circumstances that left a great deal of room for uncertainty.

AN EXCLUSIVE CONTRACT WITH MAGNUM

The other unique aspect of the making of the film was the exclusive contract signed by Frank Taylor with the Magnum photographic agency. Lee Jones, then in charge of special projects in Magnum's New York office, got in touch with Taylor as soon as she read about the project in the press. 'We met that morning,' Jones says, 'and it soon became clear that my idea that Magnum hold exclusive for all stills on *The Misfits* fit neatly Taylor's plans for the film. He wanted it to be elite and special from the outset.'[6] It would not be the first time that Magnum photographers had covered the making of a film, but it was the first time they had obtained exclusive rights, and with actors as famous as Monroe, Gable and Clift. Lee Jones recalls: 'Magnum had worked on other films as still photographers and each time there was a painful struggle between the publicity department's needs and expectations and Magnum's basic belief that copyright belongs to the photographer. There were predictable clashes: the producers knew that a Magnum coverage had a better chance in the major magazines and Magnum felt obligated to sell first rights to whatever publication we felt would do the photographer – and the film – the greatest good. But the publicity departments were accustomed to receiving all of the work of a commercial set photographer, and to making their own choices.' The fact that Magnum won an exclusive contract owes much to Frank Taylor's personality; Jones describes him as 'a most unusual man, he understood and admired good photography'. John Huston liked photographers too. He had been a friend of Robert Capa, who founded Magnum with Henri Cartier-Bresson and George Rodger in 1947. After Capa's death, Huston retained his connections with some of Magnum's photographers, among them Inge Morath, who had covered several of his films, including *Moulin Rouge* and *The Unforgiven*, a routine Western that Huston hated. The fact that Cornell Capa, Robert's brother, was one of the photographers sent to cover *The Misfits* was bound to bring back happy memories for him.

It was agreed that Magnum would send its best photographers in teams of two, changing every fifteen days throughout shooting. Dick Rowan, an editor in the New York office, would also stay in Reno to write the captions, once permissions had been obtained from the actors, who had contractual rights over the choice of photographs. The pictures could then be sold to newspapers and magazines all over the world. The producers wanted exclusive rights over the work of photographers who were ranked among the world's best. They

*Clockwise from top right:* Bruce Davidson and, seated, Elliott Erwitt BRUCE DAVIDSON
Evelyn Moriarty ERICH HARTMANN
Eve Arnold ERICH HARTMANN
Angela Allen and, lying down bottom right, Dennis Stock. BRUCE DAVIDSON
Henri Cartier-Bresson and, in front, Montgomery Clift INGE MORATH
Inge Morath and Clark Gable HENRI CARTIER-BRESSON
Ernst Haas BRUCE DAVIDSON

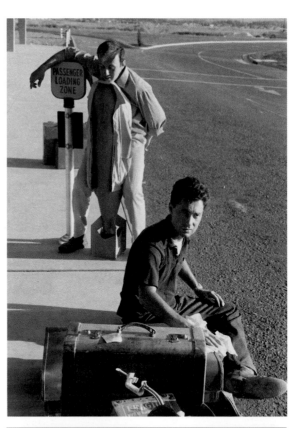

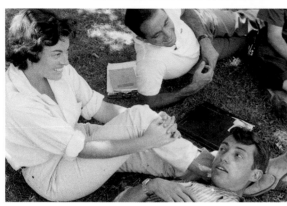

could well imagine that the presence of Marilyn Monroe, Clark Gable and Montgomery Clift would arouse great interest on the part of the American and foreign press. John Huston's personality, the fact that Miller would be with Marilyn while the film was being made, even the unusual idea of filming in the middle of the desert, would all create an aura of excitement. Also, as Eve Arnold, one of the photographers who was to cover the shoot, put it, the agreement with Magnum 'was calculated to take the burden of having to relate daily to different photographers from the shoulders of the actors. It was done particularly to free Marilyn of all extraneous concern.'[7]

Inge Morath and Cartier-Bresson were the first photographers to go to Reno, where the film crew had set up and where the first scenes were to be shot. Then came Dennis Stock, Eve Arnold, Ernst Haas, Cornell Capa, Bruce Davidson, Elliott Erwitt and Erich Hartmann. 'We drove from New York', recalls Inge Morath, 'because we wanted to discover America. Each photographer did as he or she liked, with no restrictions. Marilyn was obviously the main attraction, and many of our photos were used in the press at that time.'[8] She remembers the fifteen days she spent on the set as a unique time: 'It was definitely the most fascinating film I've ever worked on, a very intense experience. You could easily see Marilyn was causing problems; she was always late, which was no fun for the others, and the film was falling behind schedule. But when she arrived, everyone was so pleased to see her!'

Cartier-Bresson, who only worked on this one film-shoot, recorded his impressions in a taped interview. In it he describes his strange meeting with

Marilyn when he arrived at the shoot. He had never met her before, and was sitting in the cafeteria one evening, next to an empty place. It was reserved for Marilyn, who was late. She arrived, and was introduced to Cartier-Bresson, who had put his Leica on the seat next to his own. Marilyn hesitated for a moment, waiting for him to move it. Then Cartier-Bresson had the audacity to ask her to bless the camera. The story goes that Marilyn did this with a good grace, lightly brushing the Leica as she made to sit down. 'I saw her bodily – Marilyn – for the first time', he confided, 'and I was struck as by an apparition in a fairytale. Well, she's beautiful – anyone can notice this, and she represents a certain myth of what we call in France "la femme éternelle". On the other hand, there's something extremely alert and vivid in her, an intelligence. It's her personality, it's a glance, it's something very tenuous, very vivid, that disappears quickly, that appears again.' Inge Morath also emphasizes Marilyn's photogenic quality: 'Once she was ready [to be photographed], she would surpass the expectations of the lens. She had a shimmering quality like an emanation of water, and she moved lyrically.' Elliott Erwitt, who had covered the making of Billy Wilder's *The Seven Year Itch* and had photographed the famous scene where her white dress billows up in the draught from a subway ventilation grille, says, 'She loved photographers and the camera was crazy about her. Personally, I don't think she was especially beautiful, but in the end it didn't matter what she really looked like. It was hard to take a bad photo of her.'[9]

Along with Sam Shaw, Eve Arnold was without a doubt the photographer who had the most privileged relationship with Marilyn. She records that 'at photo sessions, she was in total control, she manipulated everything – me, the camera … She knew a lot about cameras and I had never met anyone who could make them respond the way she did. So she got what she wanted, because she wasn't under all the kinds of pressure she felt during a film-shoot: remembering her lines, enduring hours of preparation … With me, she was in charge of the situation.'

When describing their impressions of a film-shoot, set photographers often repeat the same theme: the waiting, which sometimes becomes very tedious. They have to wait for the perfect moment, when everything has been rehearsed, the light is ready, and everyone, actors and technicians, is in the right place. Then they must work as discretely as possible, almost invisibly, surrounded by the film crew. On the set of *The Misfits*, there was a lot of waiting, as usual, but this time, everyone had to wait for Marilyn, too. 'She was perpetually late,' says Elliott Erwitt, 'or else she didn't show up at all. It was total chaos. This is what gives the photographer so much freedom to work. Photographs are always more interesting when the subjects are taken offguard or not quite where they should be.' Eve Arnold goes further when she says, 'the big gossip was always, Would Marilyn work that day?', adding that Marilyn, who had come back exhausted from making *Let's Make Love,* had admitted to her, 'I'm thirty-four years old. I've been dancing for six months … I've had no rest, I'm exhausted. Where do I go from here?'

Dennis Stock had special responsibility within the Magnum team for photographing Montgomery Clift. 'The choice of photographers was pretty

72

'I saw her bodily – Marilyn – for the first time and I was struck as by an apparition in a fairytale.'
HENRI CARTIER-BRESSON

random, made by Magnum and the producer according to the shooting schedule and who was available. I didn't know Clift before this shoot, but I was known to have taken a lot of pictures of James Dean and Marlon Brando. That reputation gave me a sort of link with certain actors of that sort, people who weren't from the big cities but more often from the mid-West; James Dean came from Indiana, Brando from Kansas.'[10] Ernst Haas, on the other hand, was more interested in the rodeo scenes shot at Dayton, and in the capture of the wild horses near the salt lake, scenes involving Gable, Wallach and Clift, and their stand-ins. These difficult and dangerous scenes with the wild horses were shot in October, when filming was well under way. They required hundreds of takes, some shot from above in a plane, which Guido (Eli Wallach) was supposed to be flying so that he could drive the mustangs. The two other cowboys, Gay Langland and Perce, would then do their best to catch them with their lassos. In October, the climate in the Nevada desert had changed after weeks of tremendous heat. Now the wind, cold and dust interfered considerably with the work of the crew.

Erich Hartmann was the last photographer to cover the shoot, ten days of which had to take place at the Paramount studios in Los Angeles, starting on 24 October. Huston shot several scenes there, using a back-projection method that allowed him to use his actors and give the illusion of movement by projecting images of the desert onto a screen. Hartmann's pictures reveal a rather sombre mood, and the actors show signs of fatigue. It is clear that the crew will be relieved when the shoot is over.

*The Misfits* should have begun shooting on 3 March 1960, but Hollywood actors had been on a fairly solid strike; this had held up work on *Let's Make Love*, and Marilyn was not available until early July. On 18 July, Huston shot his first scenes in Reno, 'the smallest big city in the world', as a banner hanging over Main Street put it. During the first two days he shot only some footage of the city (which he later decided to discard), to use in the title sequence, while he waited for all the actors to arrive. In one of Inge Morath's photographs, the clapperboard shows the date, while in the background, Miller and Huston seem to be location-spotting in a Reno street, scouting like two soldiers on a recce. Cartier-Bresson has captured the rapport between the director and his scriptwriter, who were clearly delighted at getting to know each other by working on the same project. One of his photographs shows Huston doing a little dance in the middle of the street, surrounded by a crowd of onlookers who are in fact extras. Some of the photographs taken by Elliott Erwitt reveal the same playful intimacy: we see the two men deep in discussion, sitting together on a set. At that stage, *The Misfits* still seemed a promising venture.

Most of the crew were staying at Mapes Hotel, which also housed a casino where Huston would go straight away to indulge his habit. The hotel provided an entire support system for the film, with several rooms or suites turned into offices or editing suites. George Tomasini and Stewart Linder in fact began editing the film at the beginning of August, and gave Huston several rough-cuts as it was being shot. Every morning, before going to the set, Huston and his co-workers would watch the rushes at the Crest Theater, two blocks from the hotel.

Clark Gable arrived from Hollywood in his silver Mercedes coupé, a magnificent vehicle with gull-wing doors, in which he had promised himself he would break speed records on his way to the set every morning. Marilyn herself arrived from Los Angeles on 20 July and was met as she got off the plane by two hundred people, including Miller, Huston and Frank Taylor, as well as representatives of the local press. She travelled from the airport to her hotel in Taylor's convertible, and the whole town turned out to watch the parade and cheer. On 21 July, Montgomery Clift checked into Mapes Hotel, before going to Pocatello, Idaho, for a few days, to learn how to handle wild horses. While he was there, he attended a rodeo, and as he was trying to help one of the wranglers mount a bull, he was knocked over and injured his nose. It seemed as if before he even started shooting, which he was supposed to do on 12 August, he had got into role as Perce, the youngest of the three cowboys. In the film, Perce wears a white bandage round his head because of a rodeo injury.

The day after she arrived, Marilyn shot her first scene, the one in which she appears at the window of the house belonging to her landlady, Isabelle (Thelma Ritter), before going to the courthouse for her divorce hearing. When shooting started, the mood seemed idyllic. On 24 July, Frank Taylor and his wife Nan gave a party at the house they had rented near Reno,

'Clark Gable arrived from Hollywood in his silver Mercedes coupé, a magnificent vehicle with gull-wing doors, in which he had promised himself he would break speed records on his way to the set every morning.' EVE ARNOLD

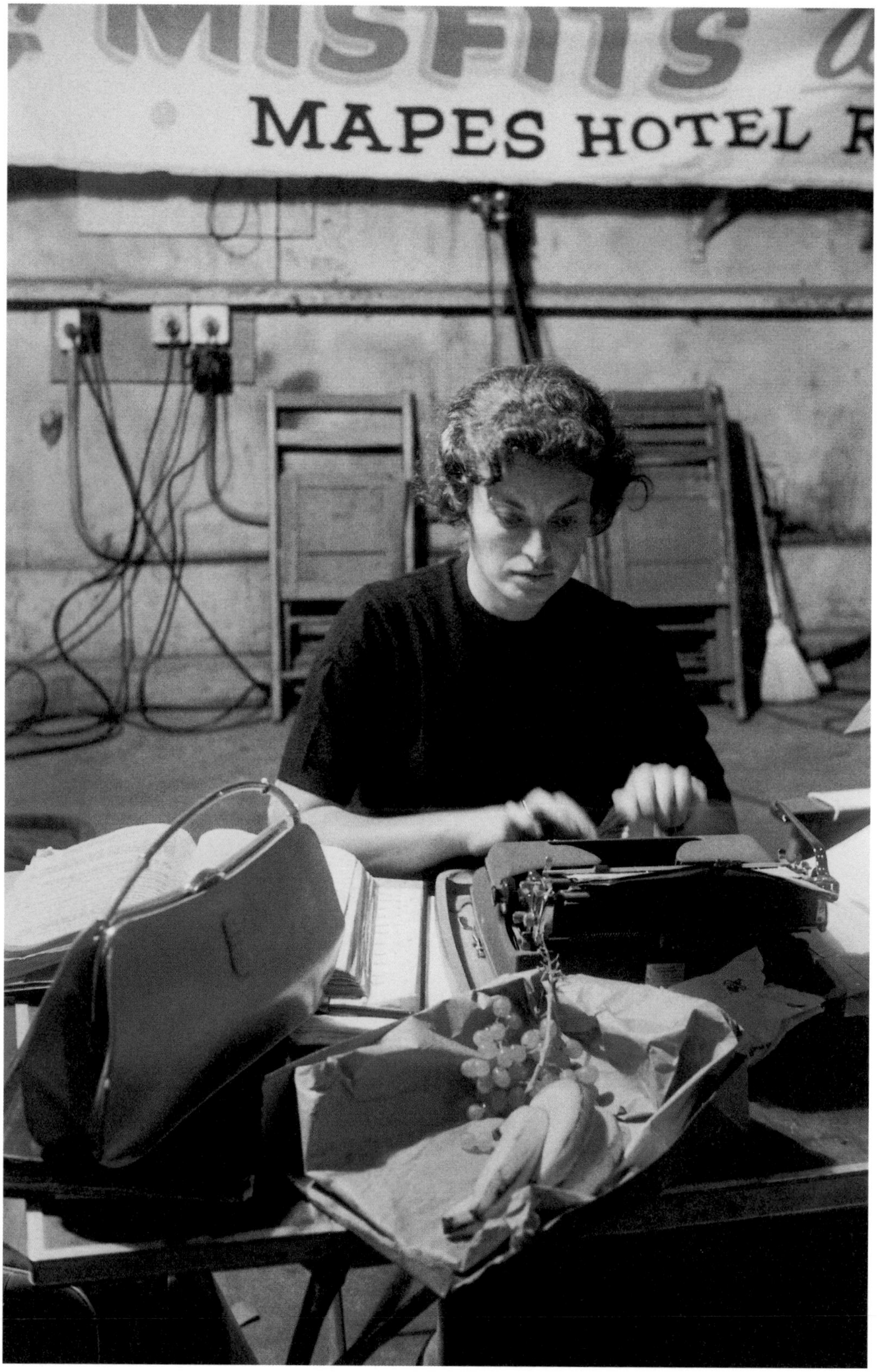
MISFITS
MAPES HOTEL

attended by all the actors, as well as by Inge Morath and Henri Cartier-Bresson. All this scrupulously detailed information appears in a diary written by James Goode, a journalist present throughout the shoot. When the film was released, Goode published a book, *The Making of The Misfits*,[11] authorized by the producers. Reading his diary, we are able to follow the shoot day by day, to note the problems, conflicts and delays and get an objective and disinterested vision of the actual process of making the film.

But it was not long before the situation on the set became intolerable, and not only on account of the sweltering Nevada heat, or the habit Marilyn had developed of arriving late on the set every day. Never free from self-doubt, and taking one kind of medication after another, she took refuge behind Paula Strasberg, who had a very strong hold over her. Strasberg was under contract to the production as Marilyn's 'coach', but in fact she played the role of intermediary between the actress and the rest of the crew. She was a kind of authoritarian guru, with the presumption to tell Huston the 'real' way he should direct Marilyn. 'She protected her like a mother hen, and dealt with all kinds of things for her,' reports Dennis Stock. This was calculated to irritate Huston and, even more, Miller. In the photographs of the shoot, Paula is always dressed in black, wearing dark glasses and a hat to protect her from the sun. In his autobiography, Miller is quite hard on the woman whom the crew 'promptly named ... Black Bart, or just Bart. Between takes, she would retire with Marilyn to her trailer, where when I entered, they would usually fall silent, just as they would before Huston.' When shooting moved to

79

At the end of the shoot, at Paramount Studios, Angela Allen, the script supervisor, with a farewell banner provided by Mapes Hotel, Reno. ERICH HARTMANN

Pyramid Lake, where the temperature was verging on 120 degrees Fahrenheit, Strasberg is said to have sat in her air-conditioned Cadillac, making Marilyn rehearse her dialogue. To counteract what he saw as Strasberg's harmful influence, Huston used irony, 'listening to everything she had to tell him with a seriousness so profound as to be ludicrous'.

Knowing how difficult it was for Marilyn to get to the set on time every day, Huston delayed the start of shooting by an hour, but to no avail. Marilyn continued to arrive late, or not at all. Filming was suspended between 27 August and 6 September while she was in a Los Angeles clinic, suffering from exhaustion. But Huston still thought of her as a professional actress, faced with the challenge of playing a role worthy of her. 'She was taking pills to go to sleep and pills to wake up in the morning ... She seemed to be in a daze half the time. When she was herself, though, she could be marvelously effective. She wasn't acting – I mean she was not pretending to an emotion. It was the real thing,' Huston would later write in his autobiography.

More than anyone else, Miller hoped that by playing Roslyn, a role with 'the womanly dignity that part of her longed for', Marilyn would recover self-confidence. When filming began, almost four years had elapsed since he had created the character: a child-woman whose tragic gaze overwhelms anyone who comes near her and tries to capture her soul, but who never ceases to search the heavens for the lucky star that will bring her joy. 'I hoped that by living through this role she too might arrive at some threshold of faith and confidence, even as I had to wonder if I could hold on to it myself after we had both been let down from expectations such as few people allow themselves in a marriage,' he wrote. This film was to be a gift to Marilyn, something that brought them closer together. Day by day, however, it turned into a martyrdom for her, and for its begetter. In most of the photographs where we see Marilyn at Miller's side, we sense a certain indifference, even a coldness, a lack of understanding on both sides. Miller often looks as if he is present on the set as a distant observer of the crew's work. Erich Hartmann captured the writer towards the end of filming, worn out, abstracted, absorbed in his own thoughts, his own solitude. Almost miraculously, Inge Morath managed to photograph Marilyn and Miller in their Reno hotel bedroom. It is a magnificent photograph: Marilyn is looking away, out of the window, and Miller keeps a certain distance. 'Everyone wanted pictures of Marilyn and Miller together,' Morath states. 'She didn't pose with Arthur, and refused to stand beside him. So I took this photo by instinct, without thinking about their relationship.'

In many of the pictures, Marilyn is alone, her face sad, concentrating on her character or learning her lines. But she achieves a sort of gaiety (probably for the photographer's benefit, and to play a kind of game with him or her) as soon as she's with Clark Gable, Eli Wallach or Montgomery Clift, co-stars with whom she was on friendly terms, even at the worst moments. When she felt involved in the scene she had to play, her face could suddenly light up and become radiant. Whether she's happy or sad, alone or in company, anxious or

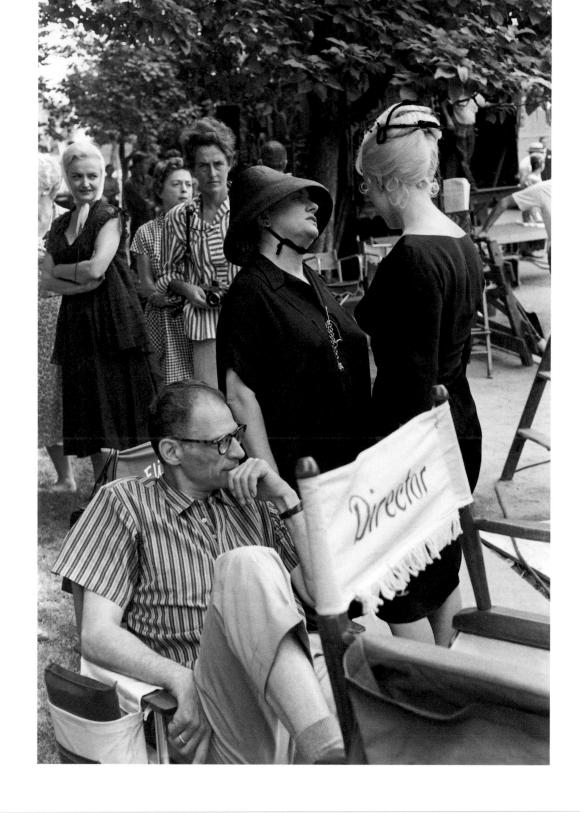

82

cheerful, wearing a genuine mask of pain or dancing as she delights in her own physicality, Marilyn's duality is what comes across most strikingly in these photographs.

In his biography of Marilyn, Donald Spoto very clearly takes her side. He confirms that because she had trouble sleeping due to stomach problems, she took tablets every night. He describes the making of the film as a kind of battle between Marilyn and the Miller–Huston duo. He is very negative about the screenplay, which, according to him, 'was full of grand but disconnected rhetoric about rugged individualism, the contemporary lack of intimacy and communication, the decline of the West and the nature of the American conscience'.[12] In his opinion, the script's main defect is that 'very little happens'. Spoto's view of the film is very narrow: *The Misfits* has nothing to do with the classic Western or with traditional genre movies. It tells the story of people who are completely 'unbalanced' – the title of the French version was *Les Désaxés*, or 'The Unbalanced' – three men and two women who form an isolated little community in the vastness of Nevada. What they have in common is a sickness, a psychological wound, a 'split' that prevents them living, and it is precisely this profound disablement that makes them so touching. They have difficulty in living in a world they cannot grasp, that no longer matches their dreams. In its own way, *The Misfits* is the story of an impossible dream, set in an America where the great myths have died. That is what Spoto refuses to see in the film. But he makes an even more radical critique when he states that Miller was settling scores with his wife by giving

Arthur Miller, Paula Strasberg and Marilyn Monroe. In the background, Marilyn's stand-in, Evelyn Moriarty, and photographer Inge Morath. HENRI CARTIER-BRESSON

her a part that in some sense became the opposite of what it had been to start with. Spoto sees Miller's conception of the character of Roslyn as full of bitterness due to the fact that his relationship with Marilyn became noticeably worse during filming. He makes much of the fact that every day Miller would rewrite the following day's dialogue, scarcely giving Marilyn time to learn her lines. This only served to increase her agitation and anxiety, and helped to make her arrive later on the set every day. According to Spoto, Miller was rewriting his script in step with every change in his marital relationship, which was deteriorating as filming proceeded. He describes this method as a kind of weapon designed to destabilize Marilyn and make her act scenes that in her own life were helping to widen the gulf between them. The problem with this view is not only that it is overly Machiavellian, but also that it relies on Miller being a *deus ex machina* controlling the very progress of the film. What is more likely is that Miller had to rewrite the script according to precise requests from Huston, who wanted to give the scenes greater fluidity, especially as he was directing the film chronologically, following the script.

But Spoto also blames Huston, whom he sees as a sadistic director who enjoyed putting his actors in danger. On the basis of the fact that he would sometimes insist on shooting several takes of a scene in the oppressive heat, Spoto concludes that Huston, with Miller's connivance, was trying to pay Marilyn back for her lateness. He goes so far as to accuse Huston of 'the decisive sabotage' of his own film, because he spent his nights playing craps

Marilyn Monroe, with her back turned, and John Huston. EVE ARNOLD

at the Mapes Hotel casino. Eve Arnold's photographs confirm this; Huston was a passionate gambler, and far from this being a secret or a hidden vice, it was part of his reputation and his legend. He refers to it freely in his memoirs: 'There was mostly craps, blackjack and roulette. Every so often a high-roller would come in, put up his bundle, get the limit raised and try to break the house. I had a marvelous time losing my ass one night and winning it back the next.' In his autobiography, Miller describes Huston with evident fascination, 'shooting craps at a table with a glass of scotch in his hand, his bush jacket as crisply pressed as if he had put it on ten minutes before. He was behind twenty-five thousand dollars. He grinned and I grinned back. It did not seem important to him, although I knew he would find it awkward paying out that much. I went up to bed. In the morning at about seven I came down for breakfast, and he was still shooting craps, still with a glass of scotch in his hand. He had won back the twenty-five grand and was now trying to win more. His bush jacket looked as neat as it had before.'

The idea that Huston and Miller were plotting against Marilyn seems implausible. What is more likely is that as work on the film proceeded, it collapsed into chaos, and that no one, neither Huston nor Miller, was able to control events. The gruelling heat, the frequent changes of location and the problems inherent in filming outdoors, the difficulties and dangers of shooting the rodeo and the capture of the horses, together with all the tensions among the crew, led to a delay of several weeks. Shooting had been scheduled to last fifty days, but was not completed until 4 November 1960, forty days late and around half a million dollars over budget. That was not the result of a cynical stratagem on the part of a director and his scriptwriter to harm the film's leading star. It was simply the reality of a shoot brought to the brink of disaster by a series of unpredictable factors.

## THE PHOTOGRAPHS AS FOOTPRINTS

The nine Magnum photographers were privileged witnesses of this venture. What is striking when one first looks at the photographs is their great variety of style, as if each photographer had been able to find a personal approach to material that was colourful in itself. They have left a record that demonstrates great freedom of vision, and none of the photographs resemble hackneyed publicity shots. On the contrary, every picture elegantly speaks of a proper detachment from the chosen subject and a genuine curiosity that is never showy or malicious. All the photographers enjoyed free access to the crew, and were able to work closely and naturally with the actors as well as with Huston, Miller and the other main players. They were part of the film's 'family', even if this family was in the process of falling apart before their eyes. But they were not aware of this at the time, and their pictures retain that true innocence that still gives them value today. They took part in the work of filming like people whose job it was to trace the 'footprints' of an individual and collective adventure in which each person's role evolved and was gradually transformed by the hazards of the weather or by personal problems.

The Magnum photographers seem to have had no wish to 'direct' their pictures, in the sense of using the actors or other leading figures on the set as

Marilyn Monroe rests between takes under the surveillance of Paula Strasberg. EVE ARNOLD

subjects from whom they could hope to extract photographic 'value added'. In fact, their pictures testify to an instinctive and spontaneous capacity to adapt to the actual realities of filming; they captured the widest possible variety of postures and attitudes using two typical patterns. The first is a photograph (or series of photographs) of the scene to be filmed or in process of being filmed that re-frames all the elements of the shot in question: see the magnificent sequences taken by Inge Morath and Dennis Stock of Roslyn dancing with Guido, those of her alone in the moonlight, dancing round the tree, or Davidson's and Erwitt's pictures of Marilyn playing paddle ball in the Dayton saloon. The second is an oblique view of a set, showing people in a variety of very diverse positions: it could be taken during time out or at rehearsal, when the actors are relaxing, concentrating hard or being made-up, or it could show various peripheral activities on the set.

The only series of photographs 'directed' by the Magnum photographers is the one in which Ernst Haas, Bruce Davidson and Elliott Erwitt try, one by one, and with visible difficulty, to get all the actors to pose together, around Miller, Huston and Frank Taylor. Taylor wanted this group photograph, no doubt for publicity purposes, even if it was just in order to preserve an 'official' image of the film: 'I was endlessly concerned about getting a group shot (Huston, Taylor, Gable, Miller, Monty Clift, Eli Wallach and Marilyn Monroe), but every time I suggested it everyone threw up their hands in horror – the thought of trying to assemble everyone seemed impossible.' In the photos taken by Ernst Haas, Huston and Gable are sitting on the rungs of ladders, while

Marilyn turns her back just at that moment. The others are absent or off-camera. One or more of the main players are missing from several of the photos in the series. But when they are all finally together, Marilyn poses in an overly obvious way (this is clearly not the kind of photo she likes or to which she gives of her best), and others move or seem uninterested in the lens, so that it is still impossible to get a 'good' group photograph. However, Elliott Erwitt had developed a stratagem. Three days previously, he had arranged a simple set – two ladders, a stool, a crate and some parachute silk – in a courtyard adjoining the Dayton saloon. 'He created enormous curiosity about it,' describes Frank Taylor, 'but refused to tell anyone what it was about. He picked a day when everything seemed to be going smoothly – he asked us all to convene – it was probably a lunch break or when we were waiting for the sun to appear from behind a cloud – he just gathered us under the silk – Marilyn and Monty were intrigued and played around and joked – it was fun and spontaneous and suddenly it was done.' But if you look at it carefully, this group photograph looks artificial, even sinister; each person is posing for him- or herself, clearly alone, indifferent to the others. Erwitt himself admits, 'Personally, I don't think it's so great. It's been seen a lot and been much in demand, but it's less interesting from the photographic point of view than for the people in it. It just so happened that everyone was available at that moment.'

In the years since 1960, the Magnum photographers have become well aware that their experience in the three months when, in turns, they lived in the

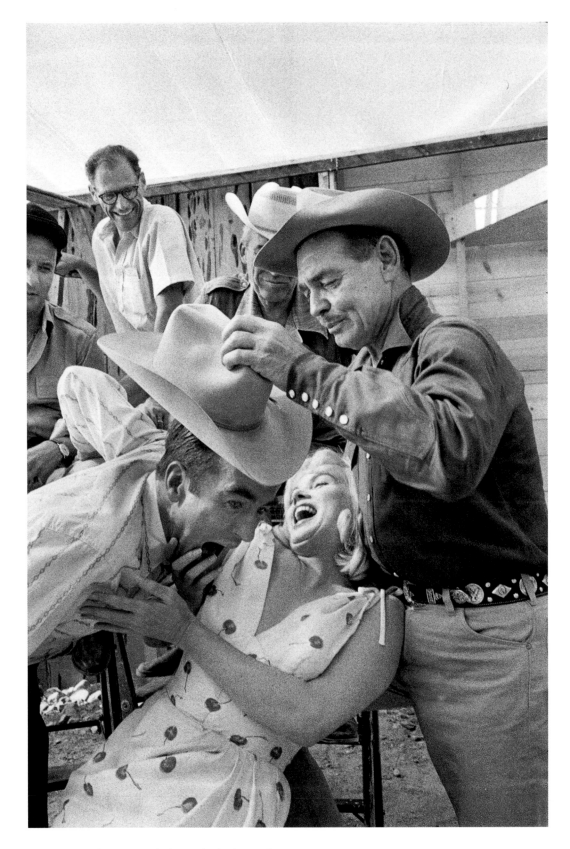

*The Misfits*: setting up the famous 'family photograph'. BRUCE DAVIDSON

*Clockwise from top left:* ELLIOTT ERWITT, ERNST HAAS, ELLIOTT ERWITT, ERNST HAAS

Nevada desert, was unique. What they did not know was that *The Misfits*, the processes of whose making they had followed closely day by day, would have such a tragic ending. In the words of Dennis Stock, 'It was one of the very last occasions when you could find that kind of intimacy between the photographers and the stars they were photographing, and this shows in the pictures. It was all like a sort of free for all, because we had nothing to lose.' As Inge Morath says, 'It also marked the end of a certain type of cinema, in which the photographers were free to move about, and take their photos using the film lighting. Today it's boring to be a photographer at a shoot; everyone wants to control their own image, everyone has their agent. A certain kind of artistic generosity has disappeared. On the set of *The Misfits*, there were still hundreds of freely available images, and that's what makes the material unique. Even Marilyn, while she did control her image, gave a lot of herself, spontaneously ... and Clark Gable, who was a big star, didn't make a big thing of it, and always made himself available to us.'

All these photographs form an invaluable visual record, capturing the lighting of the film, both of actors and landscapes, and recreating the atmosphere of a shoot. Brought together here like a jigsaw puzzle, they bear witness to a unique experience, fixing for ever each person's state of mind, their anxieties and enthusiasm and their moments of weariness and hope as a film was in the process of being made. They are like fireflies, lighting up the dark skies of people looking for their lucky star.

'It just so happened that everyone was available at that moment.' ELLIOTT ERWITT

Shooting of *The Misfits* was completed on 4 November 1960. The following day, Clark Gable had a heart attack and was admitted to hospital in Hollywood. He died on 16 November after a second attack, without being able to see the final version of the film. Montgomery Clift was already preparing to play another demanding role, Freud, for Huston. Relations between the two deteriorated to the point that the five-month-long shoot of *Freud: A Secret Passion* became a torment for Clift, an actor marked by his air of fragility and his delicate, expressive features. As soon as *The Misfits* was finished, Marilyn made public her separation from Miller. He returned alone to New York, while she was about to start a new film, *Something's Got to Give*, directed by George Cukor, which she was unable to finish. She died on 5 August 1962, in mysterious and tragic circumstances that have still not been fully explained. The image of Roslyn in *The Misfits* is thus the last we have of her on the screen. No one today can be in any doubt that it is the image of a great actress.

SOURCES

1 ARTHUR MILLER, *Timebends: A Life* (New York, 1987).
2 SAM SHAW and NORMAN ROSTEN, *Marilyn Among Friends* (London, 1987).
3 John Huston Collection, Margaret Herrick Library, Academy of Motion Pictures.
4 JOHN HUSTON, *An Open Book* (New York, 1980).
5 FRANÇOIS TRUFFAUT, *Hitchcock* (New York, 1967).
6 As told to Clélia Cohen and the author, July 1999.
7 EVE ARNOLD, *Marilyn Monroe: An Appreciation* (New York, 1987).
8 Interview with the author, 23 September 1998.
9 Interview with Alain Bergala for *Magnum Cinéma* (Paris, 1994).
10 Interview with the author, 25 June 1999.
11 JAMES GOODE, *The Making of The Misfits* (New York, 1961).
12 DONALD SPOTO, *Marilyn Monroe: The Biography* (London, 1993).

Thanks to *The Misfits*, Marilyn Monroe proved she was also a great dramatic actress. EVE ARNOLD

picture essay *by Magnum photographers*

18 July 1960, the first day of filming: John Huston and Arthur Miller on the streets of Reno. INGE MORATH

The mood during the first few days of filming was upbeat, effervescent and intense. Arthur Miller was on the set from day one, excited at the idea of working with John Huston, who, similarly, consulted him on many points. 'Arthur Miller is a joy to work with. You have a new idea and Miller comes back ten times better.' Huston first shot some footage on the streets of Reno, for the title sequence. Much later, he decided to replace it with abstract graphic titles based on the pieces of a jigsaw puzzle. The first two days were a sort of practice lap, Huston's way of 'limbering up' his 200-strong crew before Marilyn Monroe arrived on the set.

John Huston mimes the dancing movement he wants with one of the extras. HENRI CARTIER-BRESSON

21 July 1960: Marilyn Monroe's first appearance as Roslyn. HENRI CARTIER-BRESSON

John Huston surrounded by his film crew. HENRI CARTIER-BRESSON

Arthur Miller wrote the part of Roslyn for Marilyn. She is a sensitive young woman whose husband has left her and who goes to Reno to get a divorce. INGE MORATH

Roslyn and Isabelle, her landlady (played by Thelma Ritter), on the courthouse steps just before the granting of the divorce. INGE MORATH

At Harrah's Club, Roslyn meets an ageing cowboy, Gay Langland: Marilyn and Clark Gable act together for the first time. INGE MORATH

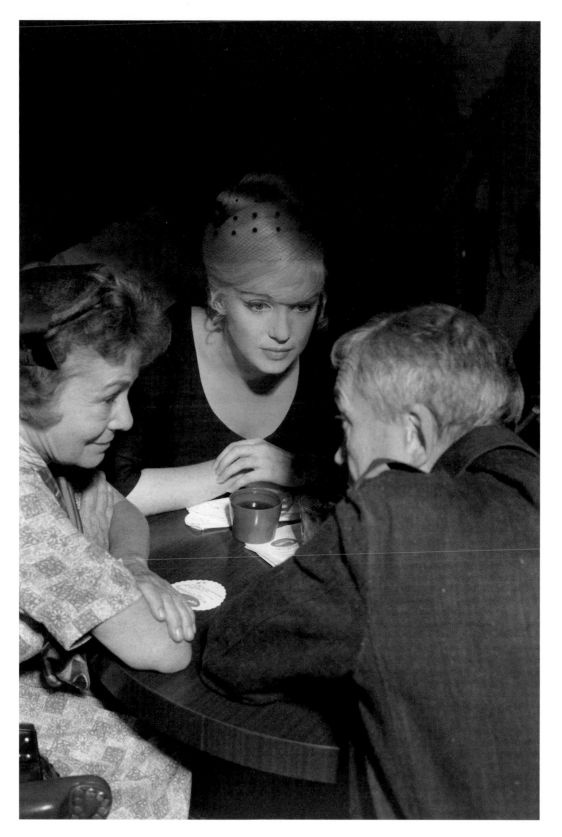

109

In spite of Marilyn's state of anxiety, Huston managed to complete the takes of this long and difficult scene a day and a half ahead of schedule. HENRI CARTIER-BRESSON

Marilyn Monroe, who has removed her shoes, walks barefoot on the earth track that leads to the ranch, followed by Eli Wallach. HENRI CARTIER-BRESSON

The shots in Reno were completed. After meeting in the bar, the characters in *The Misfits* go to the unfinished house of Guido, played by Eli Wallach. Morning and evening, the film crew, who were staying at the Mapes Hotel in Reno, travelled the fifty miles between the city and a ranch in Quail Canyon. This location, rented from a local family, was the very ranch where in March 1956 Arthur Miller had met a young woman who had come from the East to get a divorce, as well as the two cowboys who inspired the story of *The Misfits*. By this stage in filming, the days were full of uncertainty; every morning the question of whether Marilyn would work that day was on everyone's lips and the start time was put back to cover her lateness.

The Quail Canyon ranch invaded by the crew of *The Misfits*. INGE MORATH

Eli Wallach, Thelma Ritter, Marilyn Monroe and, with his back to the camera, Clark Gable. INGE MORATH

At Guido's ranch, the film's main characters stay together for a few drinks and a dance or two to music from a car radio. Eli Wallach and Marilyn launch into a brilliant sequence that is both rhythmical and languid from the effects of their drinking. It was important to Miller as it had to carry one of the story's main ideas: when people are with Roslyn, they are transformed, and her presence even casts a spell over a neglected house.

Eli Wallach: 'It was good to take Marilyn and dance with her, to take her away from Gable.' INGE MORATH

Marilyn Monroe and Eli Wallach. INGE MORATH

Marilyn made as if she was going to fall, and before Eli Wallach caught her, the entire crew held their breath.
DENNIS STOCK

117

Roslyn waking up. INGE MORATH

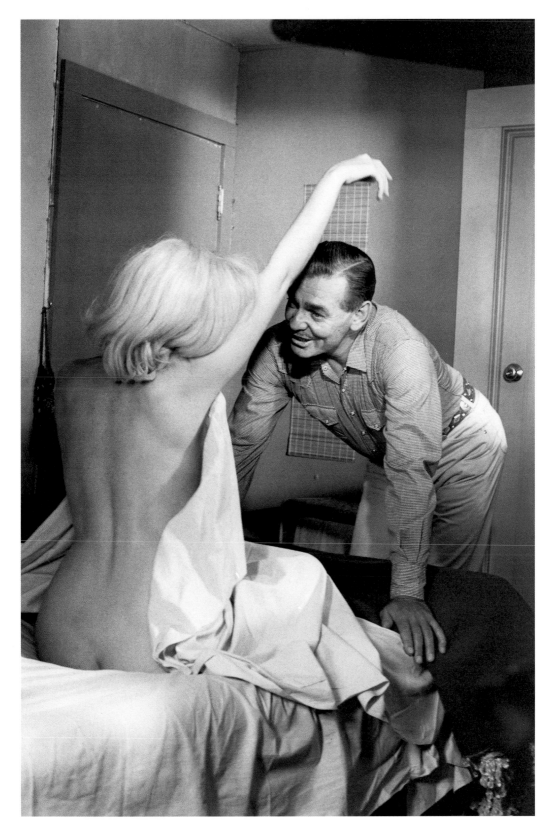

For one shot, Marilyn let a sheet slip and reveal one of her breasts. She saw this as a way of attracting a bigger audience for the film: 'Let's get the people away from television sets,' she said. In the end, Huston cut out the shot: 'I have always known that girls have breasts.' INGE MORATH

'Once she was ready [to be photographed], she would surpass the expectations of the lens. She had a shimmering quality like an emanation of water, and she moved lyrically.' INGE MORATH

'When you smile it's like the sun coming up,' Gay says to Roslyn. INGE MORATH

Marilyn dances alone in the moonlight. INGE MORATH

Dancing in the moonlight, Marilyn suggests her character's closeness to nature, the sky, the earth and the trees.  INGE MORATH

This moment of grace was seen by the censors of the day as erotic, and for a time put the film's release in jeopardy.
INGE MORATH

Between work and relaxation: Marilyn, who always found learning her lines stressful, goes over them with Paula Strasberg, while Arthur Miller talks with Eli Wallach. DENNIS STOCK

Marilyn's contract required that Paula Strasberg be there, but her presence was like a shadow looming over her relationship with Miller. DENNIS STOCK

Arthur Miller and Marilyn, who is riding away on horseback. ELLIOTT ERWITT

In mid-August, the scenes at the Quail Canyon ranch were completed. The crew then went to Dayton, where Gay and Guido take Roslyn and Isabelle. The two men have the idea of catching wild horses in the desert, and to do that they have to hire a young cowboy, whom they think they'll find at the Dayton rodeo. Montgomery Clift joined the crew to play Perce Howland, a rather vain, hot-headed cowboy with a scarred face. Because of his reputation for drinking, it was difficult to get insurance for him. However, his very first scene – a long, emotional monologue in a telephone box – was completed in a single take, and throughout the shoot Huston was impressed by his professionalism.

Arriving at Dayton, Nevada. The set designers covered the town's façades with a 'movie' version.
*Above:* DENNIS STOCK *Below:* BRUCE DAVIDSON

130

The scene where the characters arrive in town was the subject of long discussions between Miller and Huston as to what angle to choose. It needed thirteen takes before Huston was satisfied. BRUCE DAVIDSON

Montgomery Clift. DENNIS STOCK

Marilyn Monroe and Montgomery Clift; there was an immediate feeling of closeness and mutual reassurance between them.
BRUCE DAVIDSON

Marilyn with Clark Gable, James Barton (the old drunkard in the bar) and Montgomery Clift. ELLIOTT ERWITT

When Miller saw Marilyn playing with a paddle ball between takes, he had the idea of adding this scene, which later became so famous. ELLIOTT ERWITT

A relaxed moment ... BRUCE DAVIDSON

136

Montgomery Clift and Marilyn Monroe cross a street in Dayton. BRUCE DAVIDSON

*Above:* Montgomery Clift. HENRI CARTIER-BRESSON
*Below:* John Huston and Clark Gable during the rodeo scene. CORNELL CAPA

139

Montgomery Clift arrived before shooting started, and spent some time in Idaho learning rodeo skills with the help of Dick Pascoe, a cowboy who trained him and was his stand-in for scenes thought to be too dangerous.
HENRI CARTIER-BRESSON

In his first take, Monty Clift was thrown and his shirt torn. When Dick Pascoe took over for distance-shots, he too was injured, and had to leave the set for a week. ERNST HAAS

A pause while shooting at Dayton: Eli Wallach and Marilyn Monroe. ERNST HAAS

On 27 August, Marilyn, who was exhausted, left the shoot and was admitted to Westside Hospital in Los Angeles. Frank Taylor, John Huston and United Artists decided to suspend filming for a week, and the company chartered a plane to take the members of the crew to L.A. John Huston decided to stay in Reno with his editor, George Tomasini, who had started to assemble the film as shooting progressed. When the film was interrupted, the press carried rumours that relations between Marilyn and Arthur Miller were deteriorating. But when Marilyn returned, on 6 September, the whole crew seemed refreshed and ready to start again, and shooting went ahead as normal.

Frank Taylor and John Huston went to Reno airport with the crew when the shoot was interrupted. CORNELL CAPA

144

*Above:* Frank Taylor, Arthur Miller and Clark Gable. For Gable, the shoot 'turned out to be an endurance contest. You just have to keep at it.' EVE ARNOLD *Below:* John Huston. INGE MORATH

145

The wait. INGE MORATH

Montgomery Clift and Marilyn Monroe; in the background is Marilyn's stand-in, Evelyn Moriarty.  EVE ARNOLD

147

Montgomery Clift: 'When I look into her eyes, it sparks everything. To another actor, that's a joy. And it's so rare. So goddamn rare.' EVE ARNOLD

In the back room of the Dayton saloon, one take followed another. The scene between Marilyn and Montgomery Clift lasts five minutes; it is the longest in the film, and the longest that Huston had ever had to shoot. Perce Howland pours out his heart to Roslyn, describing his childhood and his loneliness. There were lapses of memory, fluffed lines and other mistakes, and each time they had to start all over again, in spite of the heat and the flies attracted by the beer cans and other rubbish that was piling up. Several days were spent on this moving scene, in which the characters project their neuroses onto each other. Huston was not happy with it, and shot it again a few days later. After Marilyn came back, the mood on the set was different, as though it had clouded over. Shooting ran over schedule and the film was still far from being finished.

149

Marilyn Monroe and Montgomery Clift shooting the longest scene in the film. EVE ARNOLD

150

That particular morning, Marilyn had surprised everyone by arriving on time. But she did not reappear after lunch, and when the time came, Monty Clift, who had actually fallen asleep on the lawn, had to be woken up. EVE ARNOLD

From the end of September, the crew drove every day to Pyramid Lake, the last

outdoor location planned for *The Misfits*. The site is an old dried-up salt lake that has

turned into a vast, bare, arid, whitish expanse surrounded by the mountains of the

Sierra. The first scenes to be shot, using 'day for night', were those in which the

characters bed down together round a camp fire the night before the capture of the

wild horses. Roslyn realizes they will be slaughtered for dog food.

153

Marilyn Monroe before shooting the camp-fire scene in the desert at Pyramid Lake. EVE ARNOLD

While they were shooting using 'day for night', Marilyn was worried about having to screw up her eyes while pretending to stare at a star Guido is describing. She said, 'That's the story of my life. Always the wrong end of the lollipop.' EVE ARNOLD

Clark Gable and Marilyn Monroe. EVE ARNOLD

155

For the scenes round the camp fire, trees and bushes were replanted round the actors and an artificial fire was lit underground, using gas.  EVE ARNOLD

A scene from the film: Roslyn abandons herself in the arms of Gay Langland. EVE ARNOLD

The film crew spent a month in the desert at Pyramid Lake, Nevada. ERNST HAAS

Towards the climax of the film – the capture of the mustangs and Roslyn's rebellion against the cowboys' brutality – everyone was drained; Huston and Miller made endless changes with the idea of improving this crucial sequence. Almost every day, Miller would give the actors new pieces of dialogue, written on scraps of paper. James Goode, the journalist who was on the set to write a detailed account of the shoot, asked Huston what justified rewriting scenes the day they were to be shot. Huston replied, 'You should think of each scene as you make it as the most important in the picture.' Marilyn was anxious about having to learn new lines, and was often absent from the set.

Marilyn prepares by herself for the important sequences at the end of the film. EVE ARNOLD

John Huston directing the scene in which Marilyn struggles with Clark Gable, who has to throw her to the ground.
EVE ARNOLD

Roslyn tries to prevent the capture of the wild horses. EVE ARNOLD

The shots of the wild horses had been taken in advance by the second crew, directed by Tom Shaw.
The actors now had to be edited into the scenes in which the horses are caught. EVE ARNOLD

*Clockwise from top left:* EVE ARNOLD, ERNST HAAS, ERNST HAAS, DENNIS STOCK, CORNELL CAPA
EVE ARNOLD, ELLIOTT ERWITT, ELLIOTT ERWITT

Although much footage had been shot in advance, the crew spent days on the actual capture. EVE ARNOLD

Every time Marilyn was unwell, they filmed the horses, as if to convince themselves that this endless shoot was not, after all, about to come to nothing. ERNST HAAS

The final weeks of filming in Nevada were particularly gruelling, and were constantly affected by adverse weather conditions. In the space of a few weeks, the desert had become autumnal and snow appeared on the mountain peaks. Every afternoon a strong wind would get up over Pyramid Lake, covering the crew and their equipment in dust and frequently forcing them to stop filming. The fine salt particles rising from the lake irritated people's eyes and throats. Filming was halted for a few days when John Huston developed bronchitis. Clark Gable was exhausted, and breathing the dust had made his voice hoarse. His stand-in, Jim Palen, sustained two serious head injuries. On 6 October, Gable sent Huston a cable saying he would agree to no further changes in the screenplay. Miller had just finished writing what he considered the best possible ending. Gable was sufficiently impressed by this final version that he agreed, one more time, to learn new dialogue.

Clark Gable was dragged along the ground on ropes tied to a lorry. EVE ARNOLD

Shadow show. ERNST HAAS

John Huston directs one of the many scenes of the capture of the mustangs. ERNST HAAS

The exterior shooting of *The Misfits* was completed at Pyramid Lake on 18 October.  CORNELL CAPA

'I never thought it would take this long,' Miller admitted to Huston at the end of the final day. EVE ARNOLD

On 24 October 1960, the whole crew was back in Hollywood, on Stage 2, Paramount Studios, to film certain scenes and some footage that required some simple special effects and back-projection. Apart from Arthur Miller and Frank Taylor, they were all in their element, the closed world of the studio, with its rules and fixed timetable. When some members of the crew left the shoot because of other commitments, they were simply replaced by other Paramount technicians. The mood was one of weary routine, very different from the excitement of the past weeks. All round the set, television studios were being built at a great rate.

175

John Huston had had salt dust brought from Pyramid Lake for the close-ups in which Gay grapples with the mustang; he handled the fake horse's hooves himself. ERICH HARTMANN

*Above:* Marilyn surrounded by the crew. ERICH HARTMANN
*Below:* Montgomery Clift, lying on the ground, replays his fall at the rodeo. ERICH HARTMANN

Stage 2 at Paramount Studios: landscape scenes of Pyramid Lake were projected onto a screen behind the aeroplane, which had been brought back from Nevada at the weekend. The same method was used for the scenes shot in cars.
ERICH HARTMANN

178

'Say Hello to me, Roslyn. – Hello, Guido.' ERICH HARTMANN

John Huston and Clark Gable in discussion at the end of the film, in Paramount Studios. ERICH HARTMANN

John Huston directing Marilyn and Eli Wallach in one of the last scenes of the film. Miller and Huston wanted Guido's ambiguousness to be more explicit, and Marilyn stayed up part of the night memorizing this new scene.
ERICH HARTMANN

'Just head for that big star straight on.' ERICH HARTMANN

Frank Taylor: '*The Misfits* is her spiritual autobiography. It's what Marilyn truly is. That's why life is so painful for her, and always will be.' ERICH HARTMANN

185

Arthur Miller: 'I still don't understand how we got to the end. I had seen this film as a gift for her, and I came out of it without her.' ERICH HARTMANN

Towards the end of the shoot, John Huston and Arthur Miller had doubts when they saw the run-through of the film for the first time and found it not entirely satisfactory. Miller got down to work again, but the problems were finally solved in the editing. ERICH HARTMANN

187

Arthur Miller: '*The Misfits* has been Clark Gable's elegy. He and Gay Langland are now one and the same person; I no longer know where one ends and the other begins.' ERICH HARTMANN

Filming of *The Misfits* was completed on 4 November 1960, forty days behind the original schedule. John Huston shot the last scene, number 269, and Clark Gable said the words that close the film: 'Just head for that big star straight on. The highway's underneath. It'll take us right home.' Huston was happy with the first take, and asked for it to be printed. Only Clark Gable and Marilyn Monroe were left on Stage 2; Eli Wallach had left for New York the previous evening, Thelma Ritter was resting at a clinic for a few days and Montgomery Clift, who had stayed in Los Angeles to see friends, was absent from the studio that day. Huston and Miller phoned Arthur Krim, President of United Artists, to tell him shooting was finished. While Marilyn was at the customary end-of-shoot party Miller went back alone in a rented car to the Beverly Hills Hotel.

'... her dream was to be a serious actress'. BRUCE DAVIDSON

the misfits

CAST
Clark Gable (*Gay Langland*)
Marilyn Monroe (*Roslyn Taber*)
Montgomery Clift (*Perce Howland*)
Thelma Ritter (*Isabelle Steers*)
Eli Wallach (*Guido*)
James Barton, Kevin McCarthy, Estelle Winwood

SCREENPLAY BY
Arthur Miller

MUSIC COMPOSED AND CONDUCTED BY
Alex North

PRODUCER
Frank E. Taylor

DIRECTOR
John Huston

DIRECTOR OF PHOTOGRAPHY: Russell Metty, A.S.C.
ART DIRECTION: Stephen Grimes and William Newberry
SET DECORATION: Frank McKelvy
FILM EDITOR: George Tomasini, A.C.E.
PRODUCTION MANAGER: C.O. Erickson
SECOND UNIT DIRECTION: Tom Shaw
SOUND RECORDING: Philip Mitchell and Charles Grensbach
SCRIPT SUPERVISION: Angela Allen
SECOND UNIT PHOTOGRAPHY: Rex Wimpy, A.S.C.
ASSISTANT DIRECTOR: Carl Beringer
ASSISTANT TO THE PRODUCER: Edward Parone
MISS MONROE'S COSTUMES BY Jean Louis
HAIR STYLING: Sydney Guilaroff and Agnes Flanagan, C.M.E.
MAKE-UP: Allan Snyder, Frank Predoha, S.M.A and Frank Larue

A Seven Arts/United Artists Production 1960
© M.G.M.

Jacket photograph: BRUCE DAVIDSON

With grateful acknowledgements to Claudine
Paquot and Agnès Sire for coordinating the
making of this book; to Eve Arnold, Alain
Bergala, James Charnock, Lee Jones, Arthur
Miller, Inge Morath, Dennis Stock and
Ouardia Teraha for all their help; to those at
the Margaret Herrick Library reponsible for
the John Huston Collection (Center for
Motion Picture Study, Los Angeles); to Clélia
Cohen for her research during the writing of
this book and for writing the captions and
commentary; to Atalante (Paris) for the layout;
to Line Martin and Derek Perrotte; and to
Imogen Forster for translating from the French.

This work was authorized by kind permission
of MGM Studios and, in particular, of its
president, Michael Nathanson. Copyright to
photographs is held by the photographers
courtesy Magnum Photos except Ernst Haas
courtesy Hulton Getty Picture Collection.

Phaidon Press Limited
Regent's Wharf
All Saint's Street
London N1 9PA

First published 2000
© 2000 Phaidon Press Limited
First published in French by
Editions Cahiers du cinéma

A CIP catalogue record for this book
is available from the British Library.

ISBN 0 7148 3936 1

Printed in France